INSPIRATIONAL THOUGHTS

(for personal growth, development and success)

INSPIRATIONAL THOUGHTS

(for personal growth, development and success)

Benjamin C. Olisa

hebron publishing
doing the King's business

Inspirational Thoughts *(for personal growth, development and success)*

by Benjamin C. Olisa

 Published by **Hebron Publishing,** 3 Egbema Close, Borikiri, Port-Harcourt, NIGERIA

Unless otherwise indicated, all Scripture quotations in this book are from the New King James Version (NKJV) of the Bible.

ISBN 978-978-785-929-2

Cover Photo:

Eyes of an African Girl by Peeterv from Getty Images Signature

Cover Concept:

Hebron Publishing

§ 1

Reading your Bible daily reloads you with wisdom that will guide you throughout the day, enabling you to face whatever challenges come your way.

§ 2

No one is ever truly alone; there are approximately seven billion people in the world, enough to keep everyone occupied—loneliness is a choice.

§ 3

Watching TV and scrolling on your phone or tablet is fun and relaxing, but completing your work can be challenging and stressful. In the end, which of these activities will pay off in the future?

§ 4

Everyone needs someone to share their story with at the end of the day. Be a good listener; it might be all they need.

§ 5

While watching football, I noticed fantastic leg drawings that are only visual to the lovers.

§ 6

There is no better way to define laziness than the word "later."

§ 7

How can you ignorantly hate someone based on what someone else told you about them, without bothering to determine whether what was told you is true or not?

§ 8

When the mind is too lazy to be creative, the body suffers the outcome and works for much less price than what it deserves.

§ 9

Keep serious people as your business partners and keep the eccentrics as your friends, because they are the ones who truly care about you.

§ 10

A woman's hair reflects her level of focus or confusion.

§ 11

Breaking up with God in difficult times is like angrily closing your bank account because the expected money has not yet arrived.

§ 12

How can the heart be wise when it is constantly exposed to folly?

§ 13

The distance between the rich and the poor is time. Do not judge people based on their current circumstances; time can change people's fortunes.

§ 14

When the heart no longer desires someone, it searches for reasons to condemn that person. But a loving heart continues to love even when there are reasons to hate.

§ 15

God does not only give us ideas; He also allows us to experience why those ideas should be implemented.

§ 16

Some questions people ask are like asking a pastor on a Sunday morning where he is going.

§ 17

Hate is a barrier that conceals the beauty of the heart and prematurely ages a person.

§ 18

A person who believes that other people's opinion is irrelevant is a fool; the wise approaches it differently.

§ 19

One of the advantages of having enlightened people as friends is that in less than an hour you can receive free lectures that took them years to study.

§ 20

No matter how skilful someone's lips are at lying, be attentive. Their actions will reveal the truth.

§ 21

Hiding your identity so that someone can accept you for who you are sounds like not being yourself.

§ 22

Some people say, "*I go to church to serve my God and then go home.*" Is that the purpose of God for the church? To avoid communicating with fellow members because of problems or feeling too superior or inferior to talk to them? Our bodies are temples of God, and keeping His commandments is worship, not just attending church. 1 Corinthians 12:25-27 emphasises that there should be no division in the body, and members should care for one another. As one body in Christ, which constitutes the church, we must renew ourselves through divine teaching from the Word of God, encouraging us to help and uplift one another (1 Thessalonians 5:11).

§ 23

If there is no love and communication within the church, what purpose does it serve to attend?

§ 24

You will not realise how good you are until you give it a try.

§ 25

You can clean a house before taking a picture in it, but you cannot do the same with a picture that has already been taken. Some things should be corrected before the damages are done.

§ 26

You do not earn people's respect by being arrogant or violent; you earn respect by respecting others.

§ 27

The real respect you seek only comes when you stop pretending and are true to yourself.

§ 28

Death is seemingly the worst thing that can happen to anyone, yet it is the only way to heaven. Without hard work and perseverance, you cannot achieve your goals or dreams in life. There are no shortcuts; do not be deceived. You only reap what you sow, and what you sow.

§ 29

We often seek miracles in many places, but there is no greater miracle than accepting Jesus Christ into your life; that's when the real miracle begins.

§ 30

Is amazing how the Holy Spirit develops our unique talents. We do not need to attend special events or schools to develop them. Yield to the Holy Spirit and follow His prodding and the purpose of your talent will be accomplished.

§ 31

Just because you do not have it now, does not mean you will not have it later. Be patient; everything will fall into place at the right time.

§ 32

We all talk about reaching our future goals and actualising our dreams, but the first and greatest goal should be entering heaven.

§ 33

If you do not feel sometimes like giving up on it, it is a hobby, not your calling.

§ 34

"Opportunity they say comes but once," but those who wait for it never experience it.

§ 35

Being judgmental and telling the truth are two different things. When people feel hurt by the truth, they often label it as judgmental.

§ 36

In the fear of speaking the truth, the truth is pushed aside, and the red line continues.

§ 37

Life truly begins when you surrender it to Jesus Christ.

§ 38

Fashion is not defined by what you wear but by the mindset of the wearer.

§ 39

There can be no fight without two or more parties involved, so, remaining quiet can create peace.

§ 40

It is okay for people to doubt your vision, but it is up to you to prove them wrong.

§ 41

When you reach the top, do not forget those who supported you and laid their backs on the floor, for you to climb to the top.

§ 42

Talent shows kill more talents than they show them.

§ 43

Talent is like a tape inside everyone that needs to be played.

§ 44

Life does not respond to our appearance but to our ability and determination to achieve our goals.

§ 45

Things that are easily obtained often lead people to undervalue them, even when what is devalued is the best they can get.

§ 46

How can one truly understand love when it is at the door but not allowed in? Many say, "I wish I could find true love," while love waits at the door, saying, "Let me in to love you."

§ 47

Having everyone is not having someone; it is another feeling when you have someone.

§ 48

Before the world can see your talent, your living room, bathroom, and kitchen would have already witnessed it, before the world can.

§ 49

I am no longer surprised when people treat me wrong; I am only surprised when someone genuinely loves me.

§ 50

A tea bag cannot release its flavour until it is steeped in hot water. Tough times bring out the best in you.

§ 51

Winning a tournament starts in the mind. When you set your mind on victory, you will push and challenge yourself to achieve.

§ 52

The more experience you gain, the fewer words you need, because people will still believe what they want to believe.

§ 53

When you have God, you have everything.

§ 54

Your current situation is not the end of your story; it is just a part of your success story.

§ 55

When someone told me I could not do it, it became the turning point of my success story.

§ 56

"For God so loved the world, that He gave His only begotten Son, that whosoever believes in Him should not perish, but have eternal life." (John 3:16).

No Jesus, no life!

§ 57

Jesus said,

> *"Come unto me, all you that labor and are heavy laden, and I will give you rest." (Matthew 11:28).*

I will never surrender to life's battles, but I surrender all to Jesus.

§ 58

It was not easy to get to where I am today, but it was worth the fight.

§ 59

In the midst of hate, show love, for love conquers all.

§ 60

Your love brings peace to my heart.

§ 61

Never marry someone out of pity.

§ 62

Today, we live in a world where speaking the truth is often seen as losing one's mind. People now prefer lies over the truth.

§ 63

What is considered "new" today will become "old" tomorrow. I remember when I used to wish for things I no longer desire. Be patient!

§ 64

Saying sorry is not a sign of weakness; it is wisdom.

§ 65

A cheating wife shames her husband, making him appear foolish before other men.

§ 66

Is it not strange how you love someone who does not love you whereas someone else out there loves you?

§ 67

Do not be saddened by someone who toyed with your heart. Just like giving a child a diamond, they toy with it because they do not know its value.

§ 68

Not every famous person possesses wisdom. Be cautious about whose advice you follow.

§ 69

Your best friends will not necessarily make you rich; sometimes strangers do.

§ 70

It is amazing how we meet strangers who become family to us.

§ 71

Sometimes life needs to stir you out of your slumber.

§ 72

A person with the right partner is much happier than having all the millions in the world but with the wrong one.

§ 73

I am not afraid of the future; I am only afraid of not spending it with you.

§ 74

A confused person has no direction, yet wonders why they have not succeeded in life. Success comes from having plans and focus. Find something you are good at, concentrate on it, and watch your dreams come true.

§ 75

Do not wish to be someone else, as you do not know what battles they are fighting.

§ 76

When you harbour hate within you, it is like being trapped behind prison gates to which you have the keys. Only you set yourself free.

§ 77

Some songs express exactly what is in your heart.

§ 78

A song may simply be a melody until life experiences add meaning to it.

§ 79

There comes a time in your life when you feel love for someone who does not reciprocate those feelings. There is often nothing you can do about it, but with time, you will move on. Each of us has someone who genuinely loves us, but we sometimes choose a more tortuous path.

§ 80

Words of wisdom are eternally fresh to those who are wise.

§ 81

The greatest reward for doing what is right is the peace it brings to our conscience.

§ 82

When a wise person spends too much time among fools, they can begin to think and act like them.

§ 83

Do not let anyone's actions or words get to you, especially when you are uncertain about their true feelings for you.

§ 84

To truly enjoy a movie, you have to watch it with a cinematic outlook.

§ 85

If ten is the highest stage in life, the most challenging number is 1—the beginning. Starting is where most people encounter difficulties. If you can initiate and persist without giving up, you will eventually reach the highest stage. So, start now.

§ 86

Love yourself with the passion that Germans love their country, and be as confident as Americans are of their nation.

§ 87

When you transition from taking risks for fun to taking calculated risks for worthy causes, you have matured.

§ 88

Often, people are busy searching for what they already possess. The answers to your questions are often right in front of you; open your eyes.

§ 89

It is challenging to communicate with people who have not experienced what you are trying to explain.

§ 90

Some songs have a unique way of understanding our inner emotions.

§ 91

Some teachers may believe they know everything and look down on students they consider less brilliant. They assume that only the ones who answer all their questions will succeed. Teachers, please remember that change is constant in life, and the students you underestimated may one day employ your "brilliant" students. My advice is to focus on your teaching and leave the judgments behind.

§ 92

Become the best version of yourself, and you will soar to new heights.

§ 93

Sometimes, all it takes to feel better is the right song playing.

§ 94

When your vision is unclear, exercise faith and proceed.

§ 95

A winner used to be a loser who never gave up.

§ 96

Never stop searching for your true self; it is what defines you.

§ 97

Do not beg for acceptance; work hard and be patient. When you next encounter those who doubted you, you will proudly say, “What was I thinking?”

§ 98

Seeing good things in your dreams does not guarantee their manifestation; it is a confirmation that through hard work, you can make them a reality.

§ 99

Your actions and attitudes toward your parents will always come back to us. So, honour and treat them well.

§ 100

If children are indeed the leaders of tomorrow, then take good care of the children around you, for you never know which leader you are nurturing.

§ 101

A wedding with its grandeur, flowers, and celebrations, is only for a few hours. What truly matters is the lifelong commitment and love you share.

§ 102

Do not marry someone because you think they are the right person; marry because you cannot imagine life without them.

§ 103

The path to the top can be lonely, with few friends along the way. However, once you reach the summit, many friends will come flocking.

§ 104

The best time of the day is when we can lay our heads on our beds to rest. This is a gift from God.

§ 105

You should refrain from boasting about how you have helped others become who they are. Recognise that God used you as an instrument to offer that help. He could have chosen anyone else, but He chose you. It is an honour, not something to flaunt.

§ 106

Every time you remind someone how you helped them, it ceases to be help; it becomes a threat.

§ 107

The two most challenging things to find in life are true love and a real family. Many people have both but are not satisfied because they believe money will make it perfect. Unbeknownst to them, what they already have is priceless.

§ 108

No one rewards you for starting something; you are only recognised when you complete your task. Stop seeking rewards from men; the real reward is from God.

§ 109

Saying "I want to have this kind of house" and "I will have this kind of house" are two different statements. If you understand this, you will start using the right words and you will rightly shape your future.

§ 110

One good idea has the potential to change your life forever. Stop complaining and start using your mind.

§ 111

Worries dissipate when you realise that life is not just about you but also about everyone else.

§ 112

When you develop the mindset of serving others, you will find satisfaction in your actions.

§ 113

Love is joy; it brings peace to the heart. Love is sacrifice; it leads one to do anything for the person they love. Love is like water; it has no enemies. Love is like fire; it can consume. Love is also pain; it can bring tears. But above all, love is the greatest thing that everyone should experience.

§ 114

Determination gives birth to success.

§ 115

Once, a wealthy man wrote in his will that his dog should inherit all his money and properties. If you measure people only by their wealth and possessions, one day you might be respecting someone's dog. Look around; many people you do not notice already respect you.

§ 116

Those who always follow others because of what they have or what they can gain often end up unhappy and with the wrong people.

§ 117

Do not boast about how good you are; let your character speak.

§ 118

God writes the songs, and we play the instruments. Regardless of the seeming insignificance of your instrument, keep playing because together, we create beautiful music.

§ 119

We are made in the image of God and should remember that He is longsuffering. We should likewise be longsuffering to inherit His promised blessings.

§ 120

Some people buy expensive designs with their money to show off, effectively advertising the designer company's products.

§ 121

Your attire attracted the kind of people who approached you. Dress honourably and honourable people will be attracted to you.

§ 122

Hope and belief keep you alive, resetting your mind daily and keeping you focused. Keep the faith; you will soon see results.

§ 123

A tree felled by the wind does not necessarily indicate weak roots but unexpected events. So, instead of asking, "Why me?" think about the way forward.

§ 124

In a world where many negative things occur, society needs more kind-hearted individuals. Be kind wherever you go, and people will miss you when you are not around.

§ 125

When at a crossroads and unsure of the path to take, you can never go wrong by choosing the right path.

§ 126

When you love someone who does not love you, it is like being hungry while looking at your favourite meal but unable to have it. When someone loves you, but you do not feel the same way, it is foolish to let go of them. When you love someone and they also love you, it is like being famished and your favourite meal is before you along with the appetite to devour it—it is a wonderful feeling.

§ 127

If you are strong, protect. If you are wise, teach. If you are wealthy, help the poor. These are gifts from God that are enhanced through sharing.

§ 128

A person is known more by their resilience during trials than by their possessions.

§ 129

Some people may appear clean on the outside but tainted within.

§ 130

People who did not believe in your dreams may one day seek your help in the very things they first doubted.

§ 131

When wise people consistently associate with foolish individuals, they might begin to believe that they are the foolish ones.

§ 132

Being successful does not necessarily demonstrate strength, but standing and persevering when down and forgotten, does.

§ 133

Those conscious of their inner abilities influence those who focus on externalities.

§ 134

In a crazy world, being normal can make you feel like you are the crazy one.

§ 135

Reading a book has the power to transform your world.

§ 136

A person without God is like a house without doors—vulnerable when life's challenges come. Many are empty without even realising it.

§ 137

A crowd with unlit candles remains in darkness. God has made you light to illuminate lives and brighten your generation.

§ 138

Many young people often seek easy solutions to life's problems; even the roads we walk on are not built without hard work. Why should the path to success be any different?

§ 139

When will people realise that relationships are private? Posting romantic pictures for the world to see reveals a phoney relationship. What then will you say to the next person? Presumably, "I never felt for them what I feel for you."?

§ 140

Some problems are not problems; how you handle them makes them problematic.

§ 141

Excessively admiring someone else's success can trap you in that state forever. Believing in yourself challenges you to be better.

§ 142

A chameleon only changes to blend into its surroundings. The niceties of human chameleons do not change who they are. Beware!

§ 143

When you think about it, money is just a piece of paper with writing on it. People place great importance on it and will do anything to obtain it. You should create your own "paper," write your goals on it, and give your best to achieve them.

§ 144

Money can buy you many things, including fake friends, love, and even marriage. However, the genuine things in life are priceless! Recognise the difference.

§ 145

Life is incomplete without love. All the money and possessions you accumulate will mean nothing in the end; only the memory of love will bring peace to your soul.

§ 146

Love is the most potent drug I know; when ingested, you cannot control or hide it.

§ 147

If you want to achieve greatness in life, you should consider serving others. When your mind is set on service, great ideas will be revealed to you.

§ 148

You cannot change what people think when they look at you, but you can change why they look at you.

§ 149

If you are rich, you will be the talk of the town while your wealth lasts. But when you touch lives, you will be celebrated for generations to come.

§ 150

Sometimes, you are holding onto things that you need to let go of so that you can see the opportunities before you.

§ 151

Some people repeatedly go through the same problem because when they ask for help or advice, they fail to explain precisely what they are experiencing. No matter how well someone may try to help, they will be unsuccessful because they will be offering a good answer to the wrong question.

§ 152

God is preparing you for something great; your testimony will prove to the world that God blesses those who diligently seek Him.

§ 153

If you stop feeling like you know everything, take a step back and listen, you might become more enlightened.

§ 154

Sometimes, life can toss you around like a washing machine. If you are not strong, it can weaken you. But if you stand strong, it will cleanse and improve you.

§ 155

Life is challenging, but the harder it gets, the stronger and better you become. The key is to never give up. Keep the faith and one day, you will be inspiring others with your story.

§ 156

There are more "zombies" than "humans" in the world today; genuine things and truth are unpopular, while trumped fake living and lies are trendy.

§ 157

When social media is no longer for showcasing your private life but for encouraging and assisting others, you will stop engaging in folly and start gaining wisdom.

§ 158

The enemy places the wrong things before you to distract you from opportunities coming your way. Stop focusing on the wrong things while the right ones pass you by. Recognise the difference.

§ 159

People may not be who you want them to be, but you can be the person you want them to be.

§ 160

Depression results from negative thoughts and wrong beliefs which are acquired and accumulated over time. Refuse negative thoughts, and rather see how God has blessed you and where He is taking you. There is a beautiful world out there; trust God and He will open you to great opportunities.

§ 161

No matter how skilled you are at what you do, if you do it where people do not value it, you may feel that you lack talent.

§ 162

I do not need an entire year to get to know you; a cup of coffee with you will reveal how you think.

§ 163

A flashy, fake person can only deceive a foolish, fake individual.

§ 164

Poverty humbles people, and the wealthy understand this. If you work for a wealthy person and believe that one day, they will give you a chance to become rich, you may be wasting your life. For who will serve them the way you do?

§ 165

In life, there are no shortcuts; you must go through the process.

§ 166

Life is a journey; whatever happens along the way is a lesson for the road ahead.

§ 167

Boxing is an analogy for life; sometimes, you face easy opponents, and sometimes, you face tough ones. Win or lose, every fight provides you with more experience making you a better fighter. So, never give up; train your mind to become a champion.

§ 168

You need to trust your inner being when it provides you with information about what is right or wrong.

§ 169

God knows what you do not know; you worry and complain because you do not know. He is silent because He knows, so trust Him and He will give you peace.

§ 170

Nobody wants a broken plate. Stop looking for someone to heal you; get healed, and the right person will come along.

§ 171

You do not call someone a failure when they are still on their journey.

§ 172

To rise to the top, you may initially have to work alone. When you prove yourself, more hands will join to make the work easier.

§ 173

If you wish to change the mistakes of the past, be ready to discard the knowledge you acquired for the future.

§ 174

If a small bulb can light up a large dark hall, then no matter how little you see yourself in this vast world, you can be a light in it.

§ 175

If we want to eliminate racism, we must eradicate the root cause. The more we focus on it, the longer it persists.

§ 176

When you are with the right team, winning becomes easier.

§ 177

A secret shared with a friend with many words is like making a public announcement.

§ 178

When a person falls at a point in their life, they vent their frustration on those they had helped who have refused to reciprocate.

§ 179

Money can make people act foolishly, yet the poor may perceive such as wisdom.

§ 180

Do not promise what you cannot deliver just to make someone momentarily feel good; it can hurt even longer later on.

§ 181

Do not promise love when you do not mean it; the repercussions can be drastic!

§ 182

Do not give up; you are almost there!

§ 183

Do not say you will not share because it is little. If you cannot share the little you have, you will not share when you have more because those who are faithful in little are faithful in much (Luke 16:10).

§ 184

Do not reject an opportunity because you think it is too great for you; accept the challenge, and the results will surprise you.

§ 185

Do not just live for the moment; live for the future.

§ 186

Do not marry solely for beauty or wealth; marry for love because it encompasses everything.

§ 187

Do not live beyond your means; it is unwise.

§ 188

Do not doubt your instincts when they tell you that something is right or wrong.

§ 189

Do not be in a relationship with someone who does not believe in your dreams.

§ 190

Do not be afraid to pursue your dreams or someone you love. Fear will lead you to regret not taking the appropriate action.

§ 191

Do not let challenges break you; they are meant to shape you for what you have asked for.

§ 192

Do not retaliate hastily against someone's negative energy; some people are going down and are seeking someone to take along with them.

§ 193

Let not impatience make you settle for less, missing out on the greater plans God has for you.

§ 194

Do not let a "too good to be true" attitude destroy the good you have been given.

§ 195

Do not force love; it brings self-inflicted pain.

§ 196

Do not be ashamed to seek help or learn something new. Do not hide in shame; gain freedom through it.

§ 197

Just because traffic is slow does not mean the road is blocked. Keep going; you are on the right track.

§ 198

The only way to get back at those who put you down is, to succeed.

§ 199

You do not need a million to start; you begin with one and count your way to millions.

§ 200

Most people never reach their goals because they are waiting for the perfect time. Make now your perfect time.

§ 201

The difference between us is that I do not think I am better than you; I mind my business, and that should not be a problem.

§ 202

Some words are like knives; they can cut a heart into pieces. Choose your words carefully; you might be hurting someone deeply.

§ 203

What makes a city beautiful are the beautiful hearts living within, not its high-rise buildings.

§ 204

If a leader is blind, his followers are vision-impaired and will not see his flaws.

§ 205

No matter how good you are at what you do, without discipline, you will never reach the top.

§ 206

When you let Jesus into your heart, you will experience unexplainable peace (Philippians 4:7).

§ 207

Do not assume that the poor lack wisdom and that the rich possess it. Though the words of the poor may be unheard, and those of the rich and famous are taken to heart, remember that the same Spirit shapes the hearts of both; be wise.

§ 208

God will place you in a tight corner to bring out the best in you.

§ 209

Some people try to put you down because they cannot handle the light within you. You may be busy trying to impress them, not realising that you do not belong in such circles.

§ 210

Your faith is your light; keep it burning, as it will guide you to your intended glory.

§ 211

Your condition today does not matter; your future success is what counts. How you invest in today will determine your world tomorrow.

§ 212

Trusting God in difficult situations is like sitting atop a bridge with a strong rope tied around your waist, ensuring your safety. Psalm 37:24 states,

> *"Though he fall, he shall not be utterly cast down; For the LORD upholds him with His hand."*

§ 213

How many angels have you encountered in your life who did not appear in white robes?

§ 214

You are busy chasing after someone who does not deserve you, while the person you deserve is out there searching for you. But you cannot see them because you are blinded by something that will never be.

§ 215

You will never use your potential if you do not overcome the fear of being wrong. Fear is the enemy; do not let it stop you in any way.

§ 216

Sometimes the enemy can be your motivation for success.

§ 217

Losers and those with nothing to lose go around looking for trouble. Learn to walk away when you encounter them.

§ 218

You need to shut your eyes and ears to negativity if you want to reach your goal.

§ 219

Alcohol takes the real you out and puts in you someone you will not be proud of the next day.

§ 220

When your mobile device is slow or less effective, you reboot it by switching it off and on. If you feel nothing is working for you now, God is rebooting you for optimal performance.

§ 221

Travel exposes you to different cultures. You get to know people for who they truly are, not what you have been told.

§ 222

Love can sometimes be funny. Someone cute and caring can be in love with you, meanwhile, you are in love with another person who does not care for you.

§ 223

I remember those days when I was sad about a particular pair of shoes that I could not afford; now no one wants them. So, do not be anxious about the new things you cannot afford now. God has fashioned us with great ideas, talents, and gifts. People will always introduce better ideas than what we have now. Fresh and more designs will always emerge, and there will come a time when you will laugh about not being able to afford them earlier. Work hard; the future is yours.

§ 224

A new car today will be old tomorrow; be patient.

§ 225

Examinations take us to new levels. You are going through one now and are about to reach a new level.

§ 226

A wrong way to defend an argument is to start a fight. When facing a challenge, what comes to mind is to engage in evil, but you are strong, so, trust God and He will see you through the challenge. He knows that you will come out with much glory, so, do not sell yourself short; you are priceless.

§ 227

One thing is guaranteed for the wicked: when they die in their wickedness, they will never escape hell, and their memory perishes with them as though they were never here. But good people leave positive memories everywhere they go and are hard to erase from people's hearts.

§ 228

Respect older people and listen when they speak because they have crossed the bridge you are currently on. Their words of wisdom will enlighten your path.

§ 229

A woman in love is more focused on it than on anything else.

§ 230

The wicked increase in power because good people keep quiet, but words have the power of fire and water. So, let us stand up courageously and speak out to quench the fire of the wicked.

§ 231

Many depend on the rich for favours. If your hope is in your fellow human being, a fool has more understanding than you. Your help should come from the Lord; He causes people to favour you. Ask Him for help.

§ 232

When your past comes knocking on your door, you do not open the door if you never invited them in the first place.

§ 233

A fool is wise in their conceit; no matter how hard you try to make them see reason, they remain bent on their folly, but being wise, you should learn to let go.

§ 234

The most dangerous enemy is the one closest to you. Because you trust and hear them always, they influence your decisions. You are your worst enemy, so do not stop yourself from going after the things you should.

§ 235

Before God gives you a sign to move, He has already prepared where you are going. So, walk by faith, not by sight, and be not afraid.

§ 236

If we act more and talk less, we can find solutions to our problems. Let us love more and talk less about how we do not love each other.

§ 237

Sometimes it is hard to let go, but when it is time to move forward, you just have to let go.

§ 238

Leave a positive footprint so that when you expire, people will not only remember you for good but will also see you living every day through the evidence of your good works.

§ 239

We sleep so long on our blessings that without challenges, we would not have gone for them. Therefore, be grateful to God for the challenge that woke you up to be desperate for change.

§ 240

A nation that lacks a wise leader will perish.

§ 241

Success is not drawn on the hand or face; it lives in the mind.

§ 242

A tree loses its leaves in winter, the process is called abscission. The tree then waits until spring to regain its glorious fresh leaves. This process can only cease if the tree is uprooted from its soil. No matter the season you are in now or the things you have lost, as long as you are still alive and breathing, nothing can stop your glorious set time from manifesting.

§ 243

People often celebrate someone's life more when they die rather than before. Show appreciation to those who have always been there for you, and do not wait until they pass away to express your gratitude.

§ 244

Stop focusing on the problems around you, only seeing them. Look! Blessings are surrounding you. Step outside your dark room and see the light.

§ 245

When one walks away from a fight, it does not mean they are afraid or weak; it means they are wise enough to know what they should really be fighting about.

§ 246

No matter how successful you think you are, there are places you will go and see that your success is still a teenager growing up. Always be humble and remember that someone is better than you in some way.

§ 247

Growing up, you were told that you could be anything you wanted in life, but life's challenges have erased this from your mind. Only the brave ones know that challenges are a ladder to success.

§ 248

Some people's loyalty has a price, and when you can no longer pay the price, they show you their true identity.

§ 249

A poor man's love letter is a sin before many women's eyes, but whatever a wealthy man does is pleasing to them.

§ 250

When two people fight and quarrel, the one who first apologises, whether they are right or wrong, shows understanding and wisdom.

§ 251

There are many stars in the sky, but I only see one; it has your name on it.

§ 252

There is a difference between being naturally royal to everyone and being royal to someone.

§ 253

When a person displays rude behaviour to others but is nice to you, expect to join the others one day.

§ 254

Many relationships are over before they even start, but some people are too blind to notice.

§ 255

On social networks, you can post what you want, and some people choose to show the world how foolish they are.

§ 256

I may not be smiling all the time, but that does not make me arrogant. I am just real enough not to put on a fake smile when I do not feel like smiling!

§ 257

A place that used to feel like home and that you remember and hurry to go to has suddenly become a place of nightmares. Why?

§ 258

A community with wise elders is better than a kingdom with a foolish king.

§ 259

A place of peace with a loving family is better than a wealthy home with no peace in it.

§ 260

Polite words can change the heart of a king while being rude will ruin your life.

§ 261

Small minds believe only in what they can see, but visionaries see the future and create reality for the small minds.

§ 262

Life is like a telescope. When you take a look through it, what future do you see? The power you give to what you see is the actualisation of it.

§ 263

Great people, in the beginning, are often seen as losers, but when the tables are turned, they become the inspiration for others.

§ 264

When a young waiter told his uncle that his new job was one of the best in town, the uncle asked why he said so. He replied that his tips each day are unbelievable. The uncle smiled and said to him, "Why settle for tips when you could be giving it?"

§ 265

If someone says, "When I marry I will change," do not believe them; people do not change overnight.

§ 266

A relationship is like a glass cup. How long it lasts depends on how you handle it. Forever it will be, depending on the care you give to it.

§ 267

The highest inspirational book in the world is the Bible. Read it, and you shall be highly inspired.

§ 268

If you always complain about a particular person's bad character, maybe you are the one who lacks understanding. Some people will not change, but you can learn how to handle them.

§ 269

Some people just need a little push to take the step that will lead to greatness. Let your words and actions inspire people around you.

§ 270

Let us trust unswervingly in God's promises; He has never failed to accomplish what He promised.

§ 271

Do not be in the world to please the world, but be in the word to change the world.

§ 272

No one is born dumb; we only lack information. You only become dumb if you have no interest in knowledge.

§ 273

If you have been sacrificing for a long time, and you give up on it, you could be at the breakthrough point, and there is no reward for unfinished work. At that moment someone else could step in and reap your years of sacrifice. Therefore, whatever kept you waiting until now is worth waiting for. Some things in life take longer because they are special, and that is why only a few people can have them.

§ 274

The trees clap their hands and dance to the melody of the wind's sound. How could they not burst into dance when the song is irresistible? Music is like the wind we cannot touch, yet we feel it each time it is played.

§ 275

We live in a generation where people pay money to go and watch a live event and end up watching it on their smartphone screens while at the venue.

§ 276

Have you ever been around someone bereft of ideas, yet when you provide one, they go against it?

§ 277

Sometimes it is hard to admit the truth, but do not forget to say "Thank you" to the person who was not afraid to tell you the truth.

§ 278

Your mind is your instrument, and how you use it determines the sound you get.

§ 279

We often pray for the will of God to be done in our lives, but do we allow His will to be done in us? You see, there are things God is trying to remove from you that you are still holding on to.

§ 280

Women are like roses; the more you shower them with love, the more they blossom and give you the best in them. But when you deny them the love they deserve, they can hurt you like a nutcracker.

§ 281

Do not let other people's bad character turn you into someone you are not; overcome them with your good character.

§ 282

One of the best gifts given to man is children; they make the world go round. Cherish them, because they are the future we see.

§ 283

Some people use others' weaknesses to make themselves strong. When someone trusts you enough to tell you their secret, and you use it against them, you should be ashamed of yourself.

§ 284

Maturity comes with time, just as talent does. In the beginning, it may look like you are not talented enough in what you are doing. But if you believe in God and work hard to develop yourself, you will become the person people cannot ignore.

§ 285

The best place to learn is not in the four corners of a university with its great intellectual lecturers. We learn best through the experiences we acquire daily.

§ 286

Success does not proclaim itself in the mouth of the holder but blows like a trumpet from the mouth of others.

§ 287

If you are looking for motivation, remember the people who said "No" to you and the ones who think that you cannot make it; prove them wrong.

§ 288

Forgiveness is not restarting a relationship, but when you give it honestly, you are free from the hate that stole your joy for so long, and it feels like a new relationship.

§ 289

Men give women flowers, and women are the flowers that beautify men's hearts.

§ 290

"I love you" is wonderful to hear, but it melts the heart when it comes from the lips of the one who holds your heart.

§ 291

Money is not intelligent enough to listen to anyone, yet it listens to hard work, productivity, and consistency. Being wise and having bright ideas does not move money either, but when hard work is involved, money becomes your servant.

§ 292

There is a big difference between missing someone and feeling lonely. When you miss someone, even when you have people around you, you still miss that person. Sometimes people mistake needing company for missing someone.

§ 293

Sometimes people's constant "No" to you is a sign of great things ahead, notifying you that you deserve better than what you plan to settle for.

§ 294

If you want to build a better future for the younger generation, the first step is to teach them how to love one another.

§ 295

You do not need to be angry or hate people because they do not believe in what you believe. If you think what you know is the best, educate them quietly on it and leave it there. Humans were created to have varied expressions, but with love and understanding, we can appreciate each other's viewpoint and create a balance that will take us in the right direction.

§ 296

A habit of praise is wisdom.

§ 297

Let your "Amen" be with faith.

§ 298

A very wealthy man had kidney cancer and had only a few months to live. His relatives, friends, and employees came to show their love and care. Some came with expensive gifts, while others entertained guests to cheer him up and show him that even in death, he was not alone. But none of their entertainment and wonderful gifts meant anything to him at that moment, nor could they take away his constant fear as the day of death drew closer. As the days went by, with death staring at him, one day, his wife's sister-in-law came to visit to encourage them. And being a believer in Christ, she said a word of prayer. Before leaving, she gave them a gift of an audio tape. Out of curiosity, his wife, who was close to her sick husband, played the tape, and there were the very words of a loving Father, who never leaves His children, no matter how deeply they have disappointed or ignored Him. The words were, *"Dear son, I have loved you with unconditional love, even though you ignored me all your life, but now I have come once again to give you another chance."*

On hearing these words, the sick man shut his eyes and muttered words of repentance, asking for God's forgiveness. There and then, he received God's forgiveness and the fear of death immediately vanished. He was now ready to meet with God!

§ 299

A service-oriented mindset is a creative one.

§ 300

If you aspire to greatness, begin by contemplating how you can serve and assist others. When your mindset is attuned to the purpose, great ideas will flow to you.

§ 301

When you commit to serving others, you create space for unimaginable resources.

www.ingramcontent.com/pod-product-compliance
Lightning Source LLC
LaVergne TN
LVHW050337160826
845677LV00014B/3651

* 9 7 8 9 7 8 7 8 5 9 2 9 2 *